China's Open Wall

edited by Festus Justin Viser
Professor of Economics
Memphis State University

MEMPHIS STATE UNIVERSITY PRESS   1972

951
8546c

73-6525
LIBRARY OF CONGRESS CATALOG CARD
NUMBER: 72-90470
ISBN 0-87870-015-3

China's Open Wall

THE M. L. SEIDMAN MEMORIAL
TOWN HALL LECTURE SERIES

MEMPHIS STATE UNIVERSITY

The M. L. Seidman Memorial Town Hall Lecture Series was established by P. K. Seidman in memory of his late brother, M. L. Seidman, founder of the firm Seidman and Seidman, Certified Public Accountants.

Publication of this sixth Series of Seidman Lectures was made possible by a gift from Mr. P. K. Seidman to the Memphis State University Press.

The M. L. Seidman Memorial Town Hall Lecture Series

Contents

Coordinating Committee

FESTUS J. VISER, Director
  Professor of Economics
  Memphis State University

FRANK R. AHLGREN
  Retired Editor
  Memphis Commercial Appeal

FRED P. COOK
  News Commentator and
    Program Director
  WREC AM-FM Radio Station

DENNIS R. HENDRIX
  President
  United Food, Inc.

MORRIE A. MOSS
  Financial Consultant
  Moss Enterprises, Inc.

MRS. ROLAND H. MYERS

ABE PLOUGH
  President
  Plough, Inc.

P. K. SEIDMAN
  Partner
  Seidman and Seidman CPA

WALTER SMITH
  Acting Vice President for
    Academic Affairs
  Memphis State University

PHINEAS J. SPARER
  Professor Emeritus
  College of Medicine
  University of Tennessee

China's Open Wall

Preface

In a few short months China became the focal point of world attention. First, in the latter part of 1971, President Nixon announced that he would make an important, precedent-shattering state visit to China in the early part of 1972. Then later in 1971, after a dramatic vote, the People's Republic of China was given the place in the United Nations formerly occupied by the Republic of China. President Nixon's state visit came in February of 1972 with the world's television cameras focused on every detail.

But there are more important reasons why China should be the subject of world attention. It is one of the most heavily populated countries in the world. With a population over 800 million, it harbors nearly one fourth of the world's population. After a long civil war, a Communist regime was established there in 1949, and its growth and development under this regime has been spectacular. In more recent years it has bickered and quarreled with its sister nation, the Soviet Union, over Communist orthodoxy as well as border matters. Most important, it is today one of the world's nuclear powers and this sobering fact must be carefully taken into account in calculating the contemporary balance of power among nations.

The Seidman Coordinating Committee decided about the time of President Nixon's announced visit to select China as the theme of the 1971-72 edition of the M. L. Seidman Memorial Town Hall Lecture series. The title *China's Open Wall* was selected to suggest the beginning of open communication between China and the western world.

The task of selecting appropriate spokesmen for the China question was not easy. The Committee wanted truly authoritative speakers who would go directly to the essence of the issues involved. At the same time it wanted a contrast of viewpoints. After considerable thought and deliberation, three names were settled upon: James C. H. Shen, the Ambassador of the Republic of China to the United States; Edwin O. Reischauer, Harvard Professor and former United States Ambassador to Japan; and Dean Rusk, Secretary of State under Presidents Kennedy and Johnson and currently Professor of International Law at the School of Law of the University of Georgia.

Ambassador Shen was born in Shanghai in 1909. He took an undergraduate degree at Yenching University in Peking and a master's degree at the University of Missouri. His early career was in journalism. He worked as a reporter on Shanghai's *China Press,* as an editor in the Central News Agency in Nanking, and as an editor of *The China Mail* in Hong Kong. For six years he was Program Director of the Rediffusion Broadcasting Company in Hong Kong.

His journalism career took him eventually into government service. For two years he was Director of the International Department of the Chinese Government Information Office. He served as Director of the Information Department of the Ministry of Foreign Affairs in Taipei and later as Director of the Government Information Office in Taipei. For two years he was Taiwan's ambassador to Australia. In 1968, he became the Vice Minister of Foreign Affairs of the Republic of China. He came to the United States as ambassador in 1971.

Professor Reischauer was born and reared in Tokyo.

He took a bachelor's degree at Oberlin and a doctorate at Harvard. In addition, he studied at the University of Tokyo, the University of Kyoto, the Sorbonne, and in China and Korea. In 1958 he became Director of the Harvard-Yenching Institute, and from 1961 to 1966 he served as the United States Ambassador to Japan, and was one of the few ambassadors there to speak Japanese fluently.

His books on the Far East include *Japan, Past and Present; The United States and Japan; Wanted, An Asian Policy.* He is coauthor of *East Asia: The Great Tradition* and *East Asia: The Modern Transformation.*

Professor Rusk was born in Georgia in 1909. He took his bachelor's degree from Davidson College in North Carolina. He was a Rhodes Scholar and as such took a master's degree at St. John's College, Oxford.

He taught at Mills College in California from 1934 to 1940. In 1946, he became Assistant Chief, Division of International Security Affairs, in the State Department. This was the first in a series of positions in the State Department that included Director, Office of United Nations Affairs, Deputy Under-Secretary of State, and Assistant Secretary of State for Far Eastern Affairs. From 1952 until he became Secretary of State in 1961 he was President of the Rockefeller Foundation.

Ambassador Shen entitled his lecture, "China's Great Wall: A Metaphorical Concept and Its Modern Implications." He discusses the great wall in terms of its history and, more important, in terms of its equivalency to what newsmen have come to call the bamboo curtain. He goes on to probe the regime of Mao Tse-tung, a regime of unprecedented tyranny, he says. But it turns out that Mao Tse-tung has feet of clay and there are good reasons why

Red China would want to pursue a course of "ping pong diplomacy."

The striking thing about Ambassador Shen's address is his contention that the power bloc in Red China may not be as monolithic as previously supposed, but the address itself should be read for insight into this far reaching contention.

Professor Reischauer in his lecture, "China and Japan: The Basic East Asian Equation," prefers to view the China question in the larger context of an East Asian problem. And the problem, he says, is like a triangle with three sets of dynamic relationships: China and the United States on one side; China and Japan on another side; Japan and the United States on the third side.

Professor Reischauer talks of the highly volatile China-United States relationship. He assesses the Nixon visit and its significance. But he goes on to describe the centuries-long relationship between China and Japan and the nagging fear that China has of Japan. Not to be overlooked is the fact that Japan economically is number three in world powers. China cannot forget this.

Volatile though these other relationships be, the Japanese-United States relationship contains, Professor Reischauer believes, a significant part of the key to the very difficult East Asian question. It implies effort and diplomatic compromise in its way just as the China-United States relationship does. Again Professor Reischauer's own essay best tells the story.

Professor Rusk's lecture is entitled "Prospective Issues in United States-Chinese Relations." He begins by summarizing the long, involved story of China starting with the Japanese aggression during the 1930s. He discusses General Stillwell's predicament in China during World War II, the long civil war that raged from 1946 to 1949, and the emergence of Taiwan as a separate and controversial entity. He goes into the Kennedy administration's attitude and into that of the Johnson administration. He points out how the situation has changed during the Nixon years and how President Nixon has moved to take advantage of the change.

The former Secretary of State then attempts to appraise the significance of the Nixon visit to China. He points out that much by way of follow-up remains to be done and this will, in the final analysis, determine just how much we realize out of the trip. He discusses the possible character of the United States-China relations in the coming decades. This is the main drive of his essay, and he makes a number of interesting and telling points.

The success of this year's series depended to a considerable extent on the members of the Coordinating Committee, expanded this year from eight to ten. These people played a strategic role in the all important task of choosing a theme for the series and selecting the speakers.

Special thanks go to Mrs. Reva Cook who so very ably handled the growing task of press publicity. Also, thanks go again to Mr. Robert Garnett, who acted as my assistant and expertly handled a formidable array of problems and details.

A special debt of gratitude is merited by Mr. P. K. Seidman, who memorializes his brother, the late M. L. Seidman, by making the series financially possible. But he goes a step further. By his personal participation in the conduct of the series, in its planning and execution, he makes his memorial all the more meaningful.

Festus Justin Viser
July, 1972

"China's Great Wall: A Metaphorical Concept
and Its Modern Implications"

Lecture One

by James C. H. Shen

The general theme of this year's series of the M. L.
Seidman Memorial Town Hall Lectures is "China's Open
Wall." The word *wall,* I take it to mean, is a figure of
speech denoting an analogy between China's old Great Wall
and the bamboo curtain now existing on the mainland
of China, and a likeness between the types of conditions
calling for such barriers. The word *open,* however, brings
in a new element which is foreign to any object or sets of
objects intended to barricade and prevent communication
and access. It signifies the existence of a situation that
permits free ingress and egress. Its use here, I believe, is
not intended as a statement of fact so much as the posing
of a question: Is China's wall open?

In the realm of international relations, for instance, it
took nations a long time to subscribe to the principle of
"freedom of the open sea." Actually, before its acceptance
there was no lack of advocates among nations as well as
publicists of the doctrine of *mare clausum* (closed sea). But

since the second half of the seventeenth century, the concept of *mare liberum* gradually gained currency. A civil society or a nation that is called "open" is free; and a free society as demonstrated by history can only be brought about in a democratic environment unfettered by oppressive rule. Today the people on the mainland of China are in the shackles of a ruthless Communist regime with their lots hanging on the vile whims and whimsicalities of its unstable leadership. If free society is to be restored to that unhappy portion of China, the regime and what it stands for will first have to be eradicated.

When the general theme of these lectures was chosen, I presume that the term bamboo curtain had been taken into consideration. Indeed, the Great Wall concept has suggested many things singularly pertinent to the conditions now existing on the Chinese mainland. It echoes well with such cold-war terms as iron curtain and bamboo curtain. Though separated by some twenty-two centuries, the Great Wall and the bamboo curtain did have a common denomination in their original purposes to prevent contacts and the flow of persons and ideas. As a cold-war term, bamboo curtain was derived from iron curtain, which is supposed to have first been used in 1904 by H. G. Wells to denote an enforced break of communication with society by an individual. The latter term in its present meaning is generally attributed to Nazi Propaganda Minister Joseph Goebbels and Sir Vincent Troubridge, as evidenced by the latter's 1945 article on "An Iron Curtain Across Europe," but it was not popularized until the late Sir Winston Churchill used it in his speech in Fulton, Missouri, in 1946.

China's Great Wall was built by Ch'in Shih Huang Ti (221–206 B.C.), the First Emperor of the Ch'in Dynasty, who assumed this title in 221 B.C., the twenty-sixth year

of his reign as Prince Cheng. His name is generally associated with the Great Wall and all the implications which
it carries. At the time of the Contending States (403–221
B.C.), the states of Yen, Chao, Wei and Ch'in, all vassals
under the enfeebled feudal system of the Chou Dynasty,
each had built a wall on its northern frontier to keep out
the Huns (Hsung-nu) and other nomadic intruders. After
the Ch'ins had destroyed the six other remaining feudal
states and unified the country, the first Emperor caused to
be built a number of links to connect these walls, an ex-
tension from the northern tip of their original territory to
that of the Chao territory and an addition of two ends to
form what was called the Great Wall (Ch'ang Cheng in
Chinese, meaning Long Wall), beginning from Lin T'ao
in the west and ending in Liaotung in the east. Since then
each successive Chinese dynasty undertook to keep it in
repair and make minor modifications. After the Ming
Dynasty (A.D. 1368–1644) was established, following the
expulsion of the Mongols from China proper, extensive
restoration work was done, and the Wall today is prac-
tically as the Mings left it. As of then and now, it starts
from Chia Ku Kuan in the west and ends in San Hai Kuan
in the east, measuring some 1,400 miles. The section which
President Nixon saw during his February 1972 visit is only
thirty-five miles from Peking.

The Great Wall has many implications bearing directly
on the kind of conditions existing on the Chinese mainland
today. First, it was designed to be a barrier, a barrier in
this case against the incursions of the nomadic tribes from
the vast northern steppes. As a defense line against external
foes, it could be considered successful during the life of
the Ch'in Dynasty, but its span was really too short to
prove one way or another. It should be pointed out, how-

ever that the enemy of the empire had turned out to be the people, people within the confines of that wall itself. In the long run it was not so successful, because time and time again the intruders were able to break through and occupy territories to the south. History has amply proved that at times the line of defense was so precarious that it had to be supplemented with diplomacy and statecraft. In fact, there were numerous intervals in Chinese history during which parts of the country were controlled by enemies from the northern steppes and northeastern regions; and, as an illustration, for one hundred and sixty-two years, from A.D. 1206 to 1368, China was under the Yuan, or Mongol, Dynasty.

Secondly, the Great Wall was created by forced labor raised by massive levies and at great sacrifice of human lives. No doubt it was a colossal monument, but erected with human blood. Like the other grandiose projects and administrative fiats of the first Emperor, it was characterized by unscrupulousness and cruelty. This description befits the collectivized programs of the Chinese Communists such as the commune system, the Great Leap Forward, and the like. But the Chinese Communists have abused the people by far more and have a greater variety of the most devilish methods of control than the Ch'in regime had.

Forced labor is an inseparable part of the Communist system of economy, but what is known as "reform through labor service" under the Chinese Communist regime has many features of slave labor far more severe than those in other Communist lands. According to a study on *The Human Cost of Communism in China,* done under the auspices of a Congressional subcommittee, the number of deaths in "forced labor camps and frontier development" from 1950 to 1970 is estimated at from 15 million to 25 million.

Furthermore, associated with the concept of the Great Wall were attempts of the first Emperor to suppress free thinking and to blot out what he and his advisers considered dangerous ideas. Two of his principal measures to that end were first, the "burning of books," that is, all books possessed by the people except works on medicine, divination, and agriculture, and historical records of the Ch'in regime itself, and second, the "burying alive of scholars" who held views different from those held by the rulers of the time. The policy of the Ch'in's was to break with the past and prohibit the people from making comparisons between the present and the past. Mao Tse-tung, however, has outdone the first Emperor. In May 1956 he initiated the so-called Hundred Flowers Movement with a subtle and insidious purpose. In the early stage the intellectuals were encouraged to air their grievances, but soon they were accused of being "enemies of the revolution." None were actually buried alive, but through a series of purges the voice of dissent has been effectively silenced just the same.

The fall of the Chinese mainland to communism in 1949–1950 is a tragedy not only to China but also to the other countries in Asia, especially to those on her periphery. Since their usurpation of political power on the mainland, the Chinese Communists have imposed on the people a regime of unprecedented tyranny. They have forced on the people an ideology and political system totally alien to the Chinese people and destroyed the traditional political and social institutions and the accepted cultural values. The family as a primary social unit, organized religion and free worship, the system of private property, to mention a few, have been badly destroyed or mutilated. The methods they have employed to accomplish their objectives are most preposterous and nefarious. The so-called Great Proletarian Cultural Revolution (1966–1969) has caused further material damage and loss of human lives in incalculable proportions.

According to the same study on *The Human Cost of Communism in China,* noted previously, communism on the Chinese mainland has cost, from 1949 to 1970, a minimum of thirty-two and a half million lives, and this figure may reach as high as sixty-two million according to other estimates. This explains the fact that there has been a continuous stream of escapees from the mainland, mostly young people born and raised since the Communist takeover who flee from the Communist yoke by swimming to Hongkong at great risk to their lives. Last year twenty thousand succeeded but a great number did not. It is pertinent to note that reports on the sufferings of the Chinese people in the hands of the Communists and the mass killings due to political liquidation, in forced labor camps and in connection with various fantastic projects such as the so-called "land reform" and the like, are hard to come by; and most of the people in this country do not seem to have sufficient information about such atrocities and casualties. It appears, too, that of late there has been a studied attempt on the part of the mass media to play down such cruel deeds in preparation for a détente with the Peking regime.

Humanitarianism is a noted characteristic of the cultural heritage of this great nation, and the history of the United States is replete with evidence that it has hardly ever failed to lift its voice in behalf of oppressed peoples in other lands. What a bewildering contrast when we compare this tradition to the current policy of seeking a rapprochement with the Chinese Communist regime in order to reduce international tensions and to bring it into the mainstream of international affairs, a policy which I am afraid will only result in strengthening its tyrannical rule over the people.

The idea of an "open wall" has suggested many other things. It has hinted at the desirability of knowing more about conditions in mainland China as well as aimed at things with far more serious consequences. It is unfortunate that China, as a result of the Communist rebellion, is presently in a dichotomous situation with one part of the country open and free and the other closed and under the yoke of Communist tyranny. In a way it is only natural that the free world would like to know more about that closed society behind the bamboo curtain. Along with this thought is the assertion that the Peking regime has been isolated by the United States and that it should be brought within the pale of the world community, irrespective of its unbecoming behavior and the resultant international censure. This assertion is at variance with facts and, besides, it has many injurious and self-defeating effects.

The barrier the Chinese Communists have built is a matter of studied policy. Like similar obstacles erected by Communist regimes elsewhere, it is intended more to keep the people from being influenced by free ideas and the thought that there is a better life beyond it than to keep the outside world guessing about the kind of conditions behind it. This has given the Communist regime a great advantage, because the free world is generally complacent, often equating the lack of reports on overt commotions with stability and attributing to the Peking regime greater power and capabilities than it actually possesses.

Ever since their seizure of the Chinese mainland enmity with the United States has been a major policy of the Chinese Communists. It was openly revealed and repeatedly hammered at in the mid-1940s, when many Americans were heaping praises on them and calling them "agrarian reformers" and "democratic revolutionaries for agrarian reform." This policy was further expressed in indignities and violations of international law and comity perpetrated by Communist cadres in 1949 against American diplomats and consular officials in China. The reason lies in the fact that, according to the logic of their ideology, imperialism is the greatest enemy of Communism and that the United States, being the most advanced capitalist country, is ipso facto the greatest enemy in the world. Moreover, they must find an enemy, real or imaginary; for tension and war psychosis would help them keep the disgruntled people under control.

As regards the allegation that the United States has isolated the Chinese Communists, it should be noted that the American foreign policy as implemented in the bilateral and multilateral treaties concerning mutual defense in East Asia and the West Pacific was conceived as a response to the critical situations arising from Chinese Communist aggression and threat, and that these pacts were concluded only after Peking's massive military intervention in Korea had begun in the fall of 1950.

If the "open wall" idea means to cajole the Chinese Communists into keeping their bamboo curtain slightly open in consideration of concessions it could lead to disastrous effects on the global cause of freedom. Ignoring concessions involving the sacrifice of principles or the negation of solemn engagements, the mere act of entreating them for accommodation would give them an advantage that will surely enhance their prestige and promote their interests. It is bound to produce an undesirable influence on the course of events in Asia, especially at this juncture when the United States is reducing its military presence in that part of the world and the surge of non-alignment on the part of the free countries there is most apparent.

In spite of the artificial barrier and the difficulty in gathering information from the Chinese mainland, there are certain fundamental facts about the Peking regime which should be reasonably well known to the West. Given the facts and a proper evaluation of them in consonance with the cause of freedom and the basic long-range interests and historical position of the United States in Asia and the West Pacific, as well as with its leadership role in the free world, it should not be difficult to arrive at a sound policy vis-à-vis the Chinese Communist regime. The United States has more "China watchers" than all the free world put together and has spent enormous sums of money from official and private sources, including academic institutions and the mass media, to gather information from behind the bamboo curtain. However, if one would recall how completely surprised this country was in the summer of 1966 when the so-called Great Proletarian Cultural Revolution was openly launched and the destructive "Red Guards" appeared on the scene, one cannot help thinking how wrong were those who had vouched for the stability of the Mao Tse-tung regime.

What then are the fundamental facts about that regime which must be clearly understood? Here I might venture, very briefly, a few observations within the little time I have at my disposal. With no claim to any profound expertise, I hope nevertheless that my comments will clear

away a little of the murky atmosphere surrounding the
Chinese Communists.

First, the regime is by no means stable; and the wav-
ing of olive branches and entreaties for a détente tend to
strengthen it and dim the hope of freedom on the part of
the people behind the bamboo curtain. As in past years,
there will be continuous crises due to popular opposition,
factionalism, and power struggle in the leadership. As of
today the top leadership in Peking could still maintain a
semblance of continuity; but this superficial appearance is
only in the apex, which is not really supported by developments in the lower echelons. The base throughout the
twenty-nine provinces, special areas and municipalities is
seething with discontent. This thin filament of continuity,
therefore, cannot be mistaken for stability.

In fact, Mao Tse-tung has been in the minority of his
party for some years. He and his close associates have been
involved in the continuous intraparty struggles during all
these years. Not long after the Korean truce people outside the bamboo curtain began to hear more and more
about the criticisms levelled at Mao himself and his policies and about more stringent control of the armed forces
and the intensification of political indoctrination. In the
autumn of 1958 Mao launched two ambitious and drastic
projects: the Great Leap Forward, and the Commune
system. By the former Mao had hoped to speed up indus-
trialization. By the latter he turned the mainland into one
vast concentration camp. When they brought great disaster
to the mainland, dissatisfaction became more widespread
and intense. The year 1959 saw the purge of General Peng
Te-huai, hero of the Korean War, and of many other high-
ranking officers, and the promotion of General Lin Piao to
the post of Defense Minister. The old military comrades of

the Long March were also affected in one way or another by measures resulting, for instance, in the abolition of military ranks, insignias and the title of marshal.

The upshot of this was that Mao Tse-tung became more and more isolated and his estrangement from his comrades wider and wider. Regular conferences, from party congress to meetings of the Central Committee and the Political Bureau, were put off *sine die* or held much later than the scheduled dates. Much against his wish and to his chagrin in 1959 Mao had to yield the position of chairmanship of state to Liu Shao-chi. It was in these circumstances that he conceived the scheme of what later became known as the Great Proletarian Cultural Revolution. Officially launched at the Eleventh Central Committee Meeting of the Eighth Party Congress in August 1966 it soon led to the massive appearance of the youthful Red Guards, whom he used to destroy both the government machinery and the party apparatus.

"Cultural revolution" was really nothing but a pretext, for much of the Chinese traditional culture on the mainland had already been mutilated by that time. The real intention of Mao Tse-tung was to purge his Communist party and the Peking regime of what he called the "revisionists" and persons "who have taken the capitalist road." The Red Guards were mere innocent tools. In them Mao saw an instrument of destruction, which he could use to accomplish his objective without having to bear all the responsibilities while he was not sure of the loyalty of the armed forces.

The resultant mass upheavals, which caused a great deal of turmoil and bloodshed and untold destruction to property, enabled Mao Tse-tung to tear down the establishment. But the price he paid was a heavy one. Even at this day he does not have a regularly constituted party behind him and his Peking regime. The disarray can be clearly seen in the difficulty he has encountered in his attempt to rebuild his apparatuses.

While the Red Guards were at the height of their rampage, orders were issued to organize "revolutionary committees" to replace the then existing party and governmental setups. These new groups were called "revolutionary three-in-one" combinations to be made up of Communist cadres including bureaucrats, members of the armed forces, and leaders of the "revolutionary masses." They were intended to perform party as well as governmental functions. This cleared the way for the makeshift Ninth National Congress of the Communist Party held in April 1969. This congress, however, was considered illegal or extra-legal in the eye of Chinese Communist law, because the delegates thereto were chosen by the revolutionary committees and not by the regular party committees. Besides, attention should be called to the fact that it took two years to organize the twenty-nine revolutionary committees of the provincial level.

Almost simultaneously with his efforts to establish the revolutionary committees as a stopgap, Mao Tse-tung issued orders in the summer of 1967 to reconstitute the party committees at all levels. In the meantime the regime widely proclaimed that as soon as the organization of the twenty-nine party committees of the provincial level was completed, a "people's congress" would be called to "elect" someone to replace Liu Shao-chi as the head of state. Only after a protracted delay were the twenty-nine party committees formed last fall, but still the regime found it unable to call the promised "people's congress." To date, there is no head of state on the Chinese mainland. This state of affairs should give the West an idea as to how deep and widespread is dissension on the Chinese mainland. Meanwhile there are a million Soviet troops on the border, posing a serious threat to the Peking regime's very existence. That is why Mao has to resort to "ping-pong diplomacy" in order to improve his bargaining position vis-à-vis the Soviet Union.

Indeed, according to Communist dogma temporary peace and even cooperation are also forms of warfare. Mao's theories provide for temporary cooperation with the bourgeoisie and alternate resort to the "strategy of peace" and the "strategy of war" depending on circumstances; but the Peking regime's policy of world revolution by violence and avowed purpose of destroying the democratic and capitalist systems remain unchanged. The free world should, therefore, stay vigilant and not succumb to the temptation of reaping short-term benefits that a détente might possibly bring. I might add, parenthetically, that the Chinese Communists are challenging alike capitalism—"U.S. imperialism"—and what they call "social imperialism," meaning the Soviet Union.

Admittedly, it is difficult to ascertain facts about the Chinese Communists; but what I have referred to a while ago will furnish some important clues to the true political situation on the mainland, which, I must stress, is still in a state of flux. It will help explain the current power struggle that has been going on there since last autumn involving General Lin Piao and other high-ranking military officers, who have simply dropped out of sight without any official explanation.[1]

[1] This lecture was given before it was reported that General Lin Piao was killed in a plane crash while attempting to escape to Moscow.

Another observation I wish to make is that it is highly essential that we know the intentions and capabilities of the Chinese Communists. Generally speaking, they have more ambitious and sinister intentions than their capabilities would warrant. Unfortunately, the West is not sufficiently aware of such intentions and has at the same time overrated their capabilities. As a result, the response of the free world is not commensurate with the realities, nor is it opportune in point of time or the order of priorities in the realm of world affairs. It has thus created a state of uncertainty, which transcends the geographical limits of Asia and is affecting the ideological alignments of the world and its power struggle.

The undue importance attached to Peking is not only limited to the material, economic, and technological aspects of things. Even such factors as leadership, cohesion, loyalty, spontaneous cooperation, skill, and popular support have been inaccurately appraised. The big population on the mainland has been equated with power, but actually it should be put on the debit side of the ledger on account of low economic production and, especially, popular grievance and resistance. As it is, the regime is not a major military power, regardless of its nuclear development; it is a power formidable enough to play havoc with its neighbors, but too deficient to pose any challenge to either of the two major power centers of the world.

To this new situation, stemming from "ping-pong diplomacy," nations in as well as outside Asia will have their own ways of response. Some of their counter-measures, I am afraid, will not be conducive to the cause of human freedom and world peace. As to us, people in the Republic of China, we are taking it, as portrayed by many press reports, with "stoical calm." We are pursuing our national

policies and goals as previously established and declared
and are redoubling our efforts in nation-building according
to the three principles of nationalism, democracy, and
social welfare enunciated by Dr. Sun Yat-sen, the father of
the Republic, in the early twenties. In Taiwan we are
striving to continue our endeavors in economic construction
and social betterment and in further developing a free and
prosperous society by generally accepted democratic pro-
cesses. The modest accomplishments we made in recent
years have assured us that we are on the right road and
we are ready to share our experience with other developing
countries if they should be interested. Today we consider
ourselves as trustees of the Chinese people. We are not only
the repository of the Chinese culture, but also a beacon of
hope for all freedom-loving Chinese, including our oppressed compatriots on the mainland. In spite of the vicis-
situdes in recent years, we remain a viable democratic force
in Asia, and will continue to make our contributions to the
cause of freedom and peace.

Between the United States and the Republic of China
there persist a continuity of friendship, a reservoir of good-
will, and many affinities associated with our common interests in building a better world order. We were allies in
two world wars and are now allies in the post-war era. At
this time of dynamic changes in the readjustment of the
international equilibrium between constructive and destructive forces, it is indeed gratifying to note that the leadership in Washington and President Nixon himself have
repeatedly assured us that the United States Government
will not forsake an old friend and will be guided by high
principles and honor its commitments.

For many years one of the basic assumptions of American foreign policy in Asia has been that, since China

occupies the central position in East Asia and has an enormous population, whatever happens in China will vitally affect her neighboring countries and ultimately the peace and security of the world. It is, therefore, in the interest of the United States to help bring about "a united, stable, strong and democratic China." But the kind of China contemplated cannot possibly be the Communist regime now in temporary control of political power on the Chinese mainland.

According to a generally accepted definition, a state is any body of people occupying a definite territory and politically organized under one government. The first two elements, people and territory, have remained the same on the Chinese mainland, and the only difference is that the governing machinery there has been in the hands of the Communists. We believe that the Communist government will not be there indefinitely. In Chinese history, a despotic regime never lasted very long. The Ch'in Dynasty, which built the links to the Great Wall, lasted only twelve years after it had unified the country by intrigue and violence.

After twenty-one years of inhuman suppression of the Chinese people on the mainland there is still a great underground of opposition to the tyrannical rule of the Peking regime. It is an underground which has been encouraged and kept alive by heroic anti-Communists from Taiwan who risk their lives to operate on the mainland. The vast majority of the people on the mainland have not accepted communism. They are waiting for daybreak.

Returning to the subject of China's wall and the question of how to "open" it, as apparently desired by some people, the proper approach, it seems to me, is not just to seek a partial lifting of the bamboo curtain or to keep it up for a while. For as long as the Communist regime is allowed to remain on the Chinese mainland, there will be impelling needs on its part to isolate the people from the outside world. The Chinese Communists must maintain that barrier of secrecy, censorship, and isolation, which as we have seen, has not only prevented the people from contact with the outside world, but also has sheltered their regime from access and detection of the true conditions behind it. Only when a free and democratic rule holds sway on the Chinese mainland once again can China's wall be kept open. We, therefore, must direct our efforts to the fundamental task of removing the underlying causes. One of the principal goals of my government is to restore freedom and democracy to the Chinese mainland. The task is admittedly difficult and we have no illusions about it. But it is a matter of faith, for faith has made man free.

Lecture Two

by Edwin O. Reischauer

Thank you very much President Humphreys; ladies and gentlemen. It's a great honor to be asked to participate in this year's Seidman Memorial Lectures, particularly in such outstanding company as the distinguished ambassador from the Republic of China, Ambassador Shen, and my old boss, Secretary Rusk. I call Mr. Rusk my old boss because I can assure you that during the five and a half years I was Ambassador to Japan I was very much aware of the fact that he was the next man up the line.

It is a great pleasure to be here in Memphis, not only because it is such a beautiful spring day, looking all the more alluring to a refugee like me from the long winter of New England, but also because this is my first visit to Memphis and, for that matter, to the state of Tennessee. I am ashamed to have to admit this, but I hope you will forgive me, because my specialization on East Asia and my constant travel in that direction has made me forego the pleasures of visiting parts of my own country.

The general subject of this series is China's open wall, and I have selected within that broad, though somewhat vague, topic the specific subject of "China and Japan: The Basic East Asian Equation," in an effort to draw our attention away from a narrow concentration on the current subject of chief immediate interest, which is our own relationship with China, to another aspect of the problem, that is, the relationship of China and Japan. I might in fact have called our subject today "China, the United States and Japan: The Recurring Triangle," because there is indeed a three-sided relationship, and, while our immediate interest lies in the Chinese-American side of the triangle, in many ways a more crucial relationship is that between China and Japan and the most crucial of all, the one between us and Japan.

Americans have often thought of themselves as having a very special relationship with China and at times a serious China problem. At the turn of the century, for example, the "Open Door" was our major policy slogan with regard to East Asia, and this over time grew into what we called the "China problem." But this "China problem" turned out to be in reality a Japanese-Chinese problem and a Japanese-American problem over different views of the future of a relatively weak China and different concepts of what the world should be like. It was these other two sides of the triangle that proved to be the most important. Once again today I believe that we will discover that these two sides are the more important aspects of the triangular relationship between the United States, China, and Japan.

Let me give just one illustration of the relative importance of the three sides of the triangle, as they stand today, by citing trade statistics and possibilities. Obviously, we have very little trade with China at present, but assuming that it develops and develops in a reasonably favorable way, it may amount before long to something like a hundred million dollars and then in time, to two hundred million dollars. But this is only one-tenth of what the Japanese have in trade with China or are likely to develop in the same time frame and only one-hundredth of the trade that we have with Japan. Thus, if the trade relationship between us and China is figured as one, that between China and Japan should be thought of as ten and that between Japan and the United States as one hundred. Trade, of course, is not the only way to measure international relationships, but it does give some idea of relative magnitudes.

Since recent developments in our relationship with China are of the most current interest and we are not many weeks past what was billed as the "week that changed the world," let me start with the American-Chinese side of the triangle. There can be no doubt that the President's visit to China did symbolize a great change in the world. But the change had already occurred. In fact, you might say that the week that ostensibly "changed the world" was only possible because the world had already changed.

Over the past few years the United States has shifted its attitudes toward China greatly. On the whole, this has been a very desirable shift in our thinking away from the concept that the world was bipolar, with us and our allies at one end of the pole, a monolithic communism at the other end, and in between a great area called the third world, or the less developed world, that was viewed as a sort of vacuum which would either be filled by us or else by the Communists. Because of this concept we felt that we would have to try to fill this third world vacuum, and we assumed that we had the power to do so. Such thinking in turn entailed the so-called containment of Chinese military aggression as the fundamental doctrine on which our relationship with East Asia was based.

Although we held to these attitudes for many years, we have now discovered that most of these propositions were false. Communism was not monolithic. It has fallen apart into as many national units as there are Communist countries. The third world is no vacuum, and this is the most important point. It is full of people. These people are aroused by nationalism. Being aroused by nationalism, they can employ the techniques of guerilla warfare, which are particularly effective in less developed countries, and they have proved able to frustrate any external power that tries to determine their destinies, as we found out at great cost to ourselves in Vietnam. In other words, there is no vacuum for us to fill, and since it is not a vacuum it will not be filled by the Chinese or by the Russians either. In other words, the containment of Chinese military expansionism was never the problem.

Our current change of policy has also taken into account the fact that we would be in a better position if we had equally friendly relationships with China *and* with Russia, because this gives us a little bit more leverage in dealing with both. In a long view of the world, too, it was obvious that a rapprochement with China, so that we could gradually build contacts and a dialogue with the close to a quarter of humanity that lives there, was much more important than worrying about the containment of a force that showed no signs of expanding.

The Chinese, too, have come to see things differently. They have seen that the United States was relaxing its close-in military containment of them, and meanwhile other worries have come to loom larger than anxiety about the intentions of the United States. For ten years or more they have been worried more about the Soviet Union than they have been about us, and recently they have come to worry again about Japan, which came very close to snuffing out their national existence only a little bit more than a quarter of a century ago. They see Japan as relatively much richer and potentially more powerful than she was even in her days of aggression, and quite understandably, therefore, they have begun to look upon her as potentially a greater threat to them than the United States. Having these two anxieties, they are eager to better their relations with us, because this would give them a little greater sense of security in what is probably the greatest and most lasting tension in Asia, namely, the tension between themselves and the Soviet Union, and they also hope that a rapprochement with us might be useful in trying to keep Japan from developing into a threat to them in the future.

In view of these changed attitudes, both in the United States and in China, the President, quite wisely and skillfully I believe, began to make overtures to the Chinese. He began in the field of rhetoric by using their own term for themselves, the Peoples' Republic of China, and then went on to other steps, such as the relaxation of trade barriers. They then replied by saying, "Let's play ping-pong," and it went on from there, eventually to Presidential tourism to the Great Wall.

This, of course, has all been very desirable, and it

symbolizes a great change that has taken place, but the President's visit to China has not itself produced any great new breakthrough. Some people feel that a significant new balance of power is being struck in the world, but this I do not see at all. As I pointed out, we may have gained a little more leverage in our dealings with the Russians on SALT talks [1] and the like, and the Chinese perhaps feel a little bit more secure about the long and dangerous geographic and ideological frontier they have with the Russians, but this does not mean that the balance of power in the world has been greatly changed.

My own feeling is that we no longer live in a balance of power situation like that of the nineteenth century or the first half of the twentieth. The world is much more in balance than most people realize. I say this for two reasons. First, the development of nuclear power has made war between major powers almost unthinkable, because it can only lead to their mutual destruction—a sort of double suicide. They dare not resort even to sub-nuclear warfare for fear that it will escalate to the nuclear level. The second reason is a point I alluded to earlier. The once seemingly empty parts of the world, in the sense of being so-called power vacuums, now have, through nationalism, adequate power to frustrate efforts at control from abroad. Their markets, their resources, their potential military bases, and their political loyalties cannot be manipulated by external military power. As a result, the great powers are not enticed into such blatant competition with one

---

[1] This lecture was delivered before President Nixon's visit to Moscow and the resultant agreement on the limitation of nuclear arms.

another as they once were over these less developed parts of the world.

There is a good illustration of this point, I believe, in the recent war in the Indian subcontinent. The Soviet Union favored one side; we and the Chinese favored the other. We grimaced at each other, and the United States even sent a task force into the Indian Ocean, but history flowed on with no reference to what the great powers were doing. The outcome was determined by basic forces within Bangladesh, India, and Pakistan, and was not significantly influenced by outside power. The fact that we lined up on the opposite side from the Russians suggests that we were motivated by desires to limit their influence over the Indian area, and, if this is true, then we clearly have no concept of what the world today is all about. The Indians are deeply nationalistic and certainly will see to it that the Soviet Union does not have undue control over them. We do not have to worry about that. And if India and Bangladesh were to become really dependent on the Soviet Union, however improbable this may be, I cannot think of anything that would put a more disastrous burden on the Soviet Union.

The old-fashioned balance of power, even if it once existed, is certainly not the world we live in today, and it is entirely unrealistic to think that there is a "balance of power game" going on in which the great powers will choose up sides, with us and the Chinese, for example, on one side and the Russians and the Japanese on the other. The relationships between the United States, China, and Japan that I mentioned earlier, which have the proportions, at least in trade, of one, ten, and one hundred, are not in any sense symmetrical or interchangeable relationships. We cannot change our one hundred relationship with

Japan for a one relationship with China, nor can the
Japanese change their ten relationship with China for
their hundred relationship with us. These proportions are
the products of geography, economy, and national political
systems and thus are not susceptible to quick or easy
change.

The President's trip to China did not even change
diplomatic relationships greatly. Both sides spoke of the
"normalization" of relations, but little real progress was
made toward this desirable goal. High officials of the two
governments will meet together from time to time—as they
did before. No trade offices were opened, and trade will
grow only very slowly. Cultural relations also will be slow
in developing. The links between the two countries, though
growing slowly, remain tenuous.

Many people hoped that something would come from
the President's visit in terms of a "deal" on Vietnam, but
this was always out of the question for two reasons. The
Chinese could not make a deal with us about Vietnam
without exposing their ideological flank to the Soviet
Union, which would then accuse them of betraying their
communist brothers in Vietnam. Nor could they make a
deal that they could force on Hanoi, because the Vietnamese are no more ready to let the Chinese decide their
future than they are ready to bow to American decisions.
If there is one thing that the Vietnamese fear more than
domination by the United States, it is domination by
China. They have made their resistance to Chinese control the central theme of their history.

There is hope that sometime a useful agreement
might emerge over Korea because there our interests do
overlap, but there was no sign of this in the communiqué
that climaxed the President's visit. Korea is divided be-

tween two intensely hostile regimes that between them have more trained soldiers than the whole of Africa, or the whole of Latin America. It is a very dangerous area, and I think it is to the interests of Chinese, Americans, and also Japanese and Russians, that a war should not break out there. Perhaps some day these four powers can do something to help guarantee the peace in the Korean peninsula.

The communiqué included some statements about Taiwan which made some people feel that we had made tremendous concessions over Taiwan and the problem there was on the way to early solution, but this is a serious misconception. We made explicit what was already implicit— that we have no vital national interest in a separate Taiwan and that we have no vital national interest in the permanent presence of American military power in Taiwan. The Chinese, no doubt, were somewhat relieved to see this in writing. I believe, however, that they actually made greater concessions in accepting the status quo with regard to Taiwan, at least for the time being. They did not even mention the fact that we have a treaty of defense with Taiwan. They kept completely silent on this important point, accepting our statement that we would gradually reduce our military power there as the situation becomes less tense in the whole area.

Thus the Chinese in a sense accepted the status quo on Taiwan for the time being, and nothing in the communiqué pointed to a solution of what is the basic problem. What is the basic Taiwan problem? It is not American ambitions about Taiwan or even Japanese ambitions, as many people in Peking seem to think. It is not an old man and his government and their dream. The basic problem is fourteen million people. That's more people than live in Australia; it is more people than live in three-quarters of the nations represented in the United Nations. These people have been politically separate from China for seventy-three out of the last seventy-seven years. They have developed a very different way of life, even though they are also Chinese. They have different habits of thought, a freer society, and a standard of living that is three times or more higher than the standard of living of the people in China. They do not want to be absorbed back into China under present conditions. They constitute and have constituted for more than two decades a relatively big and quite successful unit, and I think they will go on being a separate unit for the foreseeable future.

I feel strongly that we should do nothing to try to force them to rejoin mainland China. They have a right to self-determination, and I think that we should continue trading and having cultural relations with them, so that they, like other people in the world who constitute existing, separate political units, will have a chance to decide their own future. Thus the problem goes on. It is imperative, I believe, that we do not shift from the myth we have had for the last twenty years that China did not exist to a somewhat smaller but equally absurd myth that Taiwan does not exist. No, it exists as fourteen million people, and its future was not decided by the President's trip.

I do not mean to suggest that the President's trip had no significance. As I have said, it clearly symbolized the great change that had already occurred in American and Chinese attitudes, but beyond that it was a tremendously important step forward in what is perhaps the biggest problem of mankind over the next generation or two. This is the terrible imbalance in the world between the quarter of the world's population in the industrialized nations, which have five-sixths of the world's wealth, and the three-quarters of the world's population in the less developed countries, which have the pitiful remaining one-sixth of the world's wealth. This gap is growing all the time. And yet the world is shrinking and becoming more interdependent and more complex. There is great trouble ahead for the whole of mankind unless we find ways to begin to close this gap between the privileged minority and the huge underprivileged majority. Given the constant proliferation of power—for destructive as well as constructive purposes—there may well be a political or even military blow-up in the world within a generation or two unless we make some progress on this problem.

If we do make progress on this problem, however, this means that the less developed, nonindustrialized countries are beginning to industrialize and use up the world's resources and pollute the world environment the way we and the Japanese and the Europeans do. Then we will come all the more rapidly to the great global problem of the balance between population and worldwide resources and the problem of worldwide pollution. Such problems can only be faced globally, but we have no mechanism for doing that today, no real possibility for dialogue about them. The already industrialized nations and those that are still undeveloped will have very different perspectives on these problems. We will see the need for all nations to slow down and use the world's resources more cautiously, but they will see no reason to slow down until they have caught up with our rate of using up the world's resources and polluting the environment—by which time it may be too late. This is going to be a very difficult problem, and we must develop contacts and mechanisms through which it can be handled.

Here probably lies the greatest significance of the President's visit to China. We have started contact with China, which embraces close to one-quarter of the human race and therefore a large part of this total problem. Let us hope that, over the next two or three decades, this contact will be developed until we do have real communication, and beyond that understanding and trust, on the basis of which we can develop true cooperation. Because, unless we are in the position of being able to cooperate on these global problems with the Chinese and the other peoples of the world by the year 2000, the human race will be in very serious trouble indeed.

The President's visit made a good beginning in opening initial contact. He signaled very clearly through it that we are seeking a relationship of mutual respect and equality with the Chinese. This may seem too commonplace to need comment, but it is not at all to be taken for granted. During the last hundred and fifty years the West and the countries of the non-Western world have not really had relations of mutual respect and equality. This is something very new in the world.

The Chinese for their part, too, made a good beginning in this new contact. Up until very recently they have said that they had nothing to discuss with us until we returned the stolen province of Taiwan. Instead of saying that, they were seen to be consorting with the man they had been branding as the arch villain. They did discuss many things with him at great length, and they issued a communiqué that implied very clearly that the two sides agreed to disagree but would try to move beyond their disagreements to a better understanding. That is peaceful coexistence as we understand the term and, I think, a great concession on the part of the Chinese. Yes, we have made a good start, and let us hope that we can continue it so that by the year 2000 we may have reached the point where there is a real dialogue and a possibility for cooperation on the great human problems that will be bearing down on us by then.

In the meantime, however, there are other problems. Let me now shift to the other two sides of the triangle I have talked about—the Chinese-Japanese and Japanese-American relationships. The American-Chinese relationship may be the great problem of the 1990s and the year 2000, but Japan's relations with the United States and possibly with China are the great crises of the 1970s.

Most people think of a crisis as the product of something that went wrong. In this case, it is the product of something going too right. The Japanese grew so rapidly, so explosively, that they changed many of the basic economic relationships in the world and made necessary a whole new set of attitudes between peoples. You no doubt are familiar with Japan's growth over the last fifteen years or so. It has grown on average 11 percent in real terms per year, which means a doubling of the economy every seven years. To do this they have doubled their exports every five years. Some people predict that Japan will become, in terms of production, the biggest country in the world, larger even than the United States. Herman Kahn has some rather excessive estimates of this sort, which do not seem to take into account the many reasons why the Japanese economy will start to taper off. But still, throughout the seventies and well into the eighties, Japan's economic growth will be nothing short of explosive, requiring constant readjustments, such as the one we just went through in 1971 when there were serious economic frictions between us and the Japanese and a drastic change in the exchange rate.

Changes in attitude, however, are going to be the really difficult problems. I have mentioned one change in attitude already. The Chinese, who had almost forgotten about the Japanese for twenty years, have suddenly developed a great sense of anxiety. They wonder if Japan is re-creating by peaceful economic expansion the Greater East Asia Co-prosperity Sphere that it fought to establish in World War II. They wonder if it will go on beyond that to become a major military menace again, as it was in the past. One can understand how men like Chou En-lai and Mao Tse-tung, who spent more than half of their lives under the shadow of Japanese militarism, cannot forget that Japan not so long ago was a major threat to China's very existence. Japanese-Chinese relations could become an area of vastly greater tension than American-Chinese relations ever were. The tensions would not only be between Japan and China; they would be between Japan and the other countries of East Asia, for they too remember Japan as the great conqueror.

Japan's success has forced on the Japanese, too, some profound changes of attitude. In the middle of the nineteenth century Japan was opened by the United States from its long isolation and forced to live in a very dangerous, predatory world. It had to scramble to build up the kind of industrial power and, on the basis of this, the kind of military power that would give it security from the West and eventually win a status of at least legal equality. All this Japan did with great success, and in the process began to build on a small scale an empire like those of the Western countries. Almost completely destroyed in World War II, Japan had to start scrambling all over again to try to catch up. The Japanese quite naturally have seen themselves as a relatively poor country having to work hard to catch up with the world leaders. But now they suddenly find themselves economically number three in the world. They can no longer think of themselves as a poor nation trying to catch up. In the past they have assumed that they could maintain certain restrictions around their economy while expecting the United States and other countries to be open to them. But this is no longer possible. We demand reciprocity in the relationships, and this is a hard adjustment for the Japanese to accept. They have assumed that their own economic growth was the only thing they needed to worry about, but now they suddenly realize that they are such a powerful country economically that they have to think about the world environment, particularly the economic health and growth of the less developed countries of Asia, or there may be no world for Japan to live in. They have to adopt a much more generous attitude toward the less developed nations than they have had in the past. These are big changes indeed.

Japan's growth has forced changes in attitudes on Americans and Europeans too. Ever since the world became in a sense a single great unit something over a century ago, it has been dominated by western countries and their concepts. Non-western countries participated in the world order only on western terms. Now, suddenly for the first time in history, the third largest unit in the key field of economics is a non-western country. Before long Japan may be the world's largest global trader and therefore the most important shaper of the world's future. We and the Europeans will have to adapt ourselves to the Japanese as much as we should expect them to adapt themselves to us. One wonders if we are ready for this great new stage in East-West relations. Here is a great change in attitudes that we face.

The changes are probably more difficult for the Japanese than for the rest of us. They are going through a time of great decision, and the outcome is not certain. The situation brings to mind an unhappy analogy from the past. The first phase of Japan's effort to catch up brought it by the time of World War I to the position of the dominant power in East Asia. It already had a little empire, which it was expanding at the expense of China. Then, very suddenly, all the rules changed. Woodrow Wilson announced that empires were now out of date, and that all nations would live peacefully with one another in a world of self-determination and international trade. Since the Japanese had only a little empire compared to those of the Western countries, it is surprising that they were willing to accept the new concepts, but they did. They pulled out of Shantung in China, the first country that gave up anything in China voluntarily; they withdrew their troops from Siberia, where they had been fishing in the troubled waters of the Russian Revolution; they cut back on their army; they agreed to naval limitations.

Certain things, however, went wrong in this world of peace, self-determination, and international trade. There was not much peace and even less self-determination, or equality. When the Japanese went to the Versailles Peace Conference and asked for the inclusion in the treaty of a statement of racial equality, the United States and the British Dominions imperiously brushed the suggestion aside, since they excluded Japanese immigrants on racial grounds and were afraid such a statement might imperil this policy. The United States slapped the Japanese in the face a second time in 1924 when, after sixteen years in which they had "voluntarily" restricted immigration to the United

States, we excluded them by law as being racially unassimilable.

The real collapse of the Wilsonian System, however, came with the Great Depression. As world trade shrank and restrictive economic policies proliferated, the Japanese found themselves with a little empire as compared with the continental vastnesses of the United States and the Soviet Union and the great overseas empires of the British and French, or even of such small countries as the Netherlands and Belgium. The Japanese wondered if they had been tricked. In any case, they went back to trying to acquire an empire that would be commensurate with their power and their economic needs, and this led in turn to the disaster of World War II.

I would not for a moment wish to suggest that we are going back to another world war, but we could be at an equally crucial turning point in history if the Japanese, because they think they will not receive full equality of treatment from the United States and the other countries of the West, decide to hew to an independent economic and political course.

Let us consider for a moment the decisions that the Japanese face. On the economic side, if they want to be accepted in global trade on terms of equality by the other industrialized nations they will have to give up much of their restrictionism. This would be a very considerable sacrifice for them, because in giving it up they would have to give up some of their capacity for a fine tuning of their economy. Since they have a greater capacity to control and guide their economy than does any other country in the world the sacrifice would be substantial, but it is necessary if Japan wishes to have the sort of global trade environment in which it can best prosper.

Nonetheless, the Japanese continue to have their doubts. Will the West reciprocate by being really fair to Japan? The countries of Western Europe, ever since the end of World War II, have had very restrictionist economic policies towards Japanese imports. The United States has been much more open to Japanese goods, but we have expected certain things of the Japanese that we have not asked of European industrial countries. We have asked them to place "voluntary controls" over many of their exports so that we would not be embarrassed by having to put up restrictions at our end. And when we saw ourselves in real economic trouble, as we have in recent years, we showed a much greater nervousness about Japanese goods than we did about goods from the European countries. The Japanese wonder if we are not displaying cultural, perhaps even racial, biases. Not unnaturally they wonder whether they really will be treated economically as equals by us and the Europeans if they do take down their own restrictions and give up their own controls.

The alternative, of course, is very unpleasant for them and dangerous for the world. It would mean a much more precarious economic future for the Japanese. It would also force them to concentrate much more heavily on the less developed countries, particularly those in their own part of the world. This would mean an even greater economic domination of East or Southeast Asia, raising further the anxieties of the countries in that area—not just the Chinese, but all the others as well. This would lead to a world of much greater tensions.

An even bigger question is posed in the field of military-political relations. For the past two decades Japan and the United States have had a close relationship of shared defense through the so-called Security Treaty. There have been tremendous advantages in this for Japan. It has been able to invest less in defense than any other important country in the world, which is one of the reasons why it has been able to make such amazing economic progress. The Japanese also have been able, as it were, to hide behind our defense posture and our foreign policy, so that they themselves could keep what they called a "low posture," which meant staying out of the problems of the world and concentrating on their own economic development. This is a policy they have followed with great success.

But there have also been great costs in this policy. First it has meant American bases in Japan, which have been particularly hard for Japanese to accept, both because they were for so long an isolated country and because these bases are filled with people of a very different language, a different culture, and a different race. Foreign bases constitute a vastly bigger problem psychologically for the Japanese than they do in the countries of Europe. A second great cost has been that the "low posture" Japan has maintained behind our foreign policy has been, in a sense, an admission that Japan follows America's lead—or at least so it has seemed to the Japanese public. This was a sacrifice they were willing to make for a while after the war because they felt that catching up economically was the paramount need. But now that they are the third economic power in the world, the relationship of assumed subservience to American foreign policy is no longer psychologically tenable. If defense burdens are to be shared, this must be done on the basis of real equality with us.

The Japanese, however, have very serious doubts as to whether this can be achieved. They wonder if a relationship of equality is truly possible in view of the obvious attitudes of domination and condescension on the part of

Western nations toward the rest of the world for more than a century and the revival of such attitudes on the part of America towards the Japanese because of the American victory over Japan in the war, our occupation of the country for seven years, and the heavy dependence of Japan on the United States for many years after the end of the occupation.

While the problem of shared defense lies only between Japan and the United States, the broader problem of equality involves all the Western nations. The Europeans seem even less prepared to grant Japan full equality than do Americans. For example, it was only because of constant pressure from the United States that the European countries were willing to accept Japan into the Organization for Economic Cooperation and Development, which might be called the club of the advanced industrialized nations. It is therefore not surprising that the Japanese have doubts as to whether they are going to be accepted as anything more than second-class citizens in what is still basically a western-dominated world.

A second area of Japanese doubts concerns the reliability of United States defense commitments. They see us as swinging toward isolationism, at least in our attitudes towards Asia. They wonder if this change of attitude includes them too. The wording of the Nixon Doctrine is deeply disturbing to them. A distinction between America's shared defense relationships with other advanced countries and the need to eliminate or at least minimize defense commitments to less developed countries is understandable and reasonable. Advanced countries are almost by definition stable, and they share the same general interests as the United States. This affords the basis for a very sound relationship quite different from the defense relationship possible with less developed countries, which basically are threatened by their own internal instabilities, about which outside force can do little or nothing. As a general rule, it would be best for the United States to have no defense commitments to or bases in any less developed country.

That seems like a valid distinction. But the Nixon Doctrine has been phrased in terms of Asia, as though there was something geographic about it, or cultural, or perhaps even racial. Does it mean that the United States does not feel that it can have the same relationship with Japan that it has with the United Kingdom? All along the Japanese have had worries about this, because they are very conscious of race. They ask themselves if Americans would run risks for the defense of Tokyo equal to the risks they might run for the defense of London. Most Japanese seem to think the answer is in the negative.

The Japanese thus are posing to themselves some very serious questions about their relationship with the United States and its reliability and its ability to develop a truly equal relationship, but just at this crucial time we quite heedlessly have given them a series of serious psychological blows. The one that came on 15 August 1971 was, I think, well justified in itself. The Japanese had been much too obtuse in recognizing that they would have to give us reciprocity in economic matters and that they were no longer a weak, poor country that should expect special privileges. The argument had gone on for years, and they were slow in recognizing that time was running out on them, as the United States had often pointed out. Perhaps some sort of a shock was necessary to wake them up to the realities of the situation. But not a shock at the same time that we were administering two other shocks which were much less justified.

One of these other shocks concerned a relatively small matter. This was the import quotas to the United States of a few categories of Japanese textiles. This did not constitute a major economic problem between us, but was more a political problem in the United States and also a political problem in Japan. President Nixon had made election promises to North Carolina that he wanted to live up to at the expense of the Japanese. They pointed out that they could only make these concessions at the expense of Osaka and other places in Japan and that these would be as politically painful for them as not living up to the promises to North Carolina would be for President Nixon. But we, in effect, said, "We're bigger, and you're going to have to give way on this." This rather rough treatment threw further doubts on the possibility of an equal relationship with us.

The worst of the shocks, which happened to come first on 15 July 1971 was one over China policy, and this brings me back to the beginning of the story, namely, American-Chinese relations. The rapprochement between the United States and China is something the Japanese approve of heartily. For years they have advised us to give up the containment policy, to try to seek better relations with the Chinese, and to trade with them. Such steps, they felt, would create a situation of less tension in their part of the world. Since this is exactly what we are doing, they should be very happy, but instead they are appalled by the way we went about it.

China and relations with it loom much bigger in Japanese minds than in American. They have a long history of intimate contacts with China dating back to antiquity. More recently there has been a century of Japanese adventurism in China. It and its 800 million people, lying right next door to Japan, inevitably loom large in Japanese thoughts about the future. Moreover China policy is a major area of contention in Japanese politics in a way it is not in American domestic politics. Thus the China problem is in every way a much more difficult problem for them than for us.

The Japanese have what they consider a fairly unsatisfactory relationship with China, and they blame this largely on the United States. Back in 1951-52 we insisted that they recognize the Nationalist Government on Taiwan if they wished to have the United States Senate ratify the peace treaty that would give them back their independence. This they did, though somewhat against their better judgment. The result has been their rather ambiguous present position in which, while being the best trading partners of both Taiwan and the Peoples' Republic, they recognize only Taiwan and have a deep sense of unease and dissatisfaction regarding their relationship with their huge neighbor.

For years we urged the Japanese to stay closely in step with us in facing the problem of China, and they agreed. We kept reassuring them that we would consult closely with them on all matters, and, as they approached a time of obviously difficult transition in policies toward Taiwan and China, the Japanese government repeatedly assured the Japanese people that during this difficult time of change Japan and America would stay closely in step with each other. Then when the moment of decision came, we did something very spectacular and quite unpredictable, forgetting entirely to tell the Japanese about it, much less consult with them. What we did may have been good, but the way we did it conveyed to them the idea that we really did not pay much heed to our relationship with them and were not prepared to treat Japan as a real equal. This was a terrible and lasting shock for the Japanese government and people.

Finally let us consider what is at stake in the future of the Japanese-American relationship. Some very basic things for the world are involved. If the Japanese come to the conclusion that they cannot really go on with the defense relationship with us because either it is unreliable or else it cannot be a relationship of real equality, they will have to do a little bit more on the military side than they have been doing. Imagine how very anxious Chou En-lai and the other Chinese would be if the Japanese started to rebuild their military at a more rapid rate than they have so far. The Chinese would become terribly anxious, and so also would the Koreans, the Filipinos, the Malaysians, and most of the other peoples of East Asia. This anxiety would be sensed as hostility by the Japanese and would therefore encourage them to do even more on the military side.

In this way a drift toward rearmament might be started in Japan which could carry her in time all the way to nuclear weapons. This I feel would be a great tragedy for the Japanese and for all mankind, because, if Japan, as the number three country in the world, felt that it had to go nuclear, then others down the line might feel that they had to do so also. On the other hand, if the country that is number three stays away from nuclear weapons and gains all the more international prestige and influence for not being a nuclear power, as I think would be the case, then the rest of us might in time see how really meaningless the dreadful burden of nuclear weapons is. In other words, Americans and Russians, envying the position of the Japanese, might see the wisdom of working out a way to reduce the awful financial and psychological burden of nuclear rivalry.

On the economic side, if the Japanese decide they cannot have a relationship of equality with the United States and Europe, they will probably move towards more of a regional economy, and this, too, as I have pointed out, would increase the tensions in their part of the world. It could also have even more serious repercussions. It might contribute to the breakup of the real world community as it now exists. The greatest step forward in international relations since World War II has been the development of a world community consisting of Western Europe, North America, Japan, Australia, and a few other units that have developed a kind of economic and cultural interdependence that makes war between them now unthinkable, even though these countries include most of the great warmongers of World War I and World War II, namely the Germans, the French, the British, the Americans, and the Japanese. We have made great progress in our relations with each other since those days and have established the beginning of a true world community. But that community may go to pieces if the Japanese go off in their regional way and the Europeans follow suit in their own region. If this were to happen, what chance would mankind have to face with success the great problems of the relationship between the industrialized quarter and the nonindustrialized three-quarters of humanity, which will be pressing down on us soon? We certainly will not be ready to face these problems by the time they have become acute in 1990 or the year 2000.

In summary, we might say that we face two successive great problems of East-West relations. The first is whether or not the Japanese and the rest of us can adjust to a Japan which has become a major shaper of the world's future, accepting it as a full and equal member of the community of industrialized, trading nations. If we can make this adjustment, then we will face the even bigger question of the relationship between the industrialized countries, which, with the exception of Japan, all come from a Western cultural background, and the less developed countries, which, with the exception of Latin America, are mostly non-Western and non-white. Both problems are in essence problems of adjustment in the relationship between the Western and non-Western parts of the world, and on their outcome probably rests the future of mankind.

Lecture Three

by Dean Rusk

I am deeply complimented by your invitation to deliver a Seidman Memorial Lecture under the sponsorship of Memphis State University. Please let me extend my compliments to Mr. P. K. Seidman who has generously made this distinguished lecture series available. You have already heard from Ambassador Shen of the Republic of China and my old friend, our very distinguished former Ambassador to Japan, Professor Edwin Reischauer, who have discussed with you certain aspects of the China problem. It is a great privilege for me to comment on certain additional aspects of that matter in this final lecture of the 1972 series.

One of the pleasant things about political life in this country is that when a man winds up a tour as Secretary of State he is finished. Since I am forever out of public life, perhaps I have achieved a certain amount of detachment, although I must confess that there may remain certain elements of preference and prejudice in my thinking; perhaps we can straighten some of those out during the question period when you will have a chance to put to me such pertinent and impertinent questions as you may have on your minds. With your permission, I would like to avoid a research kind of paper this evening in order to talk very informally, to give you some impressionistic, indeed, some kaleidoscopic, comments on our relations with China, recalling some of the key elements of the past and trying to raise some key questions for the future. Perhaps my remarks will reflect at least one generation's experience with the China question.

Apart from my childhood interest in China and our missionary work there in our church, my story of China begins with the seizure of Manchuria by the Japanese during my senior year in college. I think many of us, particularly the young people, sensed that this was a much more significant event than just a battle in a far off land. Secretary of State Henry Stimson apparently felt the same way, because he tried to organize some resistance to the Japanese adventure, but President Hoover and the general state of American public opinion limited his effort to what came to be called the Stimson nonrecognition policy, namely, that we would refuse to recognize the results of the seizure of Manchuria. Then we went through the dismal decade of the thirties, when Japan moved from Manchuria into north and then central and south China, occupying most of the seacoast. The League of Nations and the United States were unable or unwilling, or both, to take any effective action to bring that aggression to a close. Secretary Cordell Hull was not permitted by our Senate to make a declaration that if the League of Nations wished to impose sanctions upon Japan, the United States would not frustrate those sanctions by insisting upon our rights as a neutral country to trade with either party. We could not even go that far. In addition to not helping China in any significant way, we continued to send the sinews of war to the Japanese and some of us young people in those days picketed the scrap iron that was going to Japan and carried our signs against the oil that we were sending to assist Japanese aggression.

Then, in other parts of the world, came Hitler's remilitarization of the Rhineland and Mussolini's invasion of Ethiopia and we found ourselves on the path to World War II. The second chapter in this story would be the war years themselves. I commend to you the brilliant book recently published by Barbara Tuchman on General Joseph Stillwell and the American experience in China. But there is one key and overriding point which I think she did not quite make clear in that book—that General Stillwell was sent to China on an impossible mission. The China-Burma-India theater during the war was our lowest priority theater, over against Europe and the Pacific. General Stillwell was provided with no significant American combat forces under his command; his job was to try to stimulate the Chinese and the British Army in India to fight the Japanese as hard as possible in order to assist our own war in the Pacific. On the one hand President Chiang Kai-shek was not going to commit his forces against the Japanese because he was looking over his shoulder at the Communists, with whom he knew he would have to deal at the end of the war. He also knew his forces would have no chance against the well-supplied forces of the Japanese with the trickle of supplies we were able to get over the hump into China. Churchill, on the other hand, was not going to commit his army in India until after the defeat of Hitler, because that army was the only imperial reserve remaining to the British. So, if you hear and read about the frictions which General Stillwell had, and I was his Chief of War Plans and was very much involved with them, bear in mind that he was trying to get them to do what they simply would not do, for reasons sufficient to them, and that a degree of disappointment and frustration was built into that situation.

At the end of the war we tried our best to establish China in the thinking of the world as a great power, one of the charter members of the United Nations, one of the permanent members of the Security Council, but many of us realized that China had been deeply gashed by the more than decade of war against the Japanese, that President Chiang Kai-shek's control over his own country was extremely tenuous, that the Chinese people were weary of war and hardship and starvation. It was something of a miracle that anything called China came out of the war at all. You will remember the mission to China of George C. Marshall, whose object was to try to bring the Nationalist and Communist leaders together to form some sort of coalition which would guarantee the peace in China and give it a chance to lick its wounds and rebuild the damage of the war. But the Marshall mission was also doomed to failure because the Chinese Communist leaders, I think, clearly believed that they were under no pressure to come to any agreement, because their estimate must have been that if they persisted they would be able to take over the entire country. So, between 1946 and 1949 we saw a grim civil war in China which the Communists rather easily won, partly because the "mandate of heaven" appeared to have passed from the government of Chiang Kai-shek as far as the masses of the Chinese people were concerned;

partly because the structure of China had been torn apart by the war itself; partly because of the corruption which was to be expected under that kind of war situation; partly, of course, because the discipline and the ability of the Communist forces themselves.

At that time the United States decided not to intervene in that civil war for two very important reasons. One was the political reason that we did not believe that we should involve ourselves in a war among the masses of the Chinese people and, secondly, we did not have the means to do so. President Truman had no real choice in front of him, because by 1946 we had no division in our army that was rated ready for combat. We had no group in our Air Force rated ready for combat. Our defense budget for 1947 was supposed to come down to about ten billion dollars. And then the U.S.S.R. greatly assisted the forces of Mao Tse-tung by disregarding their wartime agreement to recognize and support the Nationalist government of China as the government of China. In the process of accepting the surrender of Japanese forces in Manchuria, they acquired large supplies of arms and munitions which they turned over to Mao Tse-tung's forces. By some miracle, considerable numbers of mainland Chinese made their way to Taiwan and established their seat of government there —but the Communists took charge on the mainland.

It is interesting to recall that when they did so the Communist leadership selected the United States as a special object of hostility. Apparently they set about, in their propaganda and in their actions, to try to erase all traces of a more than century of close and affectionate relations between the American and Chinese people. They imprisoned some of our consular officers and beat some of them up rather badly. They tried to indoctrinate the

Chinese people into an attitude of hostility towards the
schools and the hospitals and other evidences of American
friendship for China. There was no doubt at all that we
were looked upon as an obstacle by the new Communist
regime. Then came the invasion of Korea by the Chinese
Communists in 1950. There are those who say that happened simply because United Nations' forces under General
Douglas MacArthur had moved into the north and were
approaching the Yalu River and that China reacted in
terms of self-defense. On that point I have just a little
reservation based upon something we do not clearly know.
As you will recall, we took many tens of thousands of North
Korean prisoners during the Korean fighting; when we
questioned these prisoners we were told by many of them
that for several months before the launching of the North
Korean attack, the Chinese had combed their armies in
North China to find anyone of Korean nationality or
ancestry and had moved those individuals into the North
Korean forces well before the attack broke out. We may
never know the clear answer as to what role China played,
or the Soviet Union, in the aggression in Korea. In any
event, the movement of the Chinese into Korea prompted
the United Nations for the only time since 1945 to brand
a country as an aggressor; this was done with respect to
the Chinese move into Korea.

During the mid-fifties the atmosphere of the Korean
struggle persisted. It was followed by the so-called off-shore
islands crisis in which the Eisenhower administration faced
a considerable showdown with the mainland Chinese. That
kept the tension very high indeed.

When President Kennedy first took office, I had a long
talk with him about the alternatives we faced with respect
to the Peoples' Republic of China. We went over those

alternatives in considerable detail, but his decision was that he did not wish to reopen the China question. One can only speculate, but my own impression was that he was aware of the fact that he had been elected in 1960 by the slimmest of majorities, that he did not feel that he had a strong mandate from the people, and therefore he wanted to be very careful about selecting the issues on which he wished to do battle, particularly to do battle with our Congress. He used to say to us, "If you're going to have a fight, have a fight about something, don't have a fight about nothing." He had in front of him a 1956 resolution passed, I think unanimously, by the Congress, objecting to the membership of Communist China in the United Nations and objecting to our bilateral recognition of Peking. President Eisenhower had told President Kennedy that he would try to give him as much support as he could on foreign policy questions, but on one issue he would have to oppose him publicly, namely, if President Kennedy moved to bring about the seating of mainland China in the United Nations. So President Kennedy decided, since the contacts we had with Peking were not very promising, that he would not open up the question which he considered would be deeply divisive both in the Congress and among the American people in the early 1960s. That attitude on his part was strongly reinforced by our experience with the Laos Agreements of 1962. President Eisenhower's only specific advice to President Kennedy when he turned over office to him, was to put troops into Laos. When President Kennedy looked at the Laotian situation he did not like that idea very much. It was a remote landlocked country where the lines of communication were very poor. More importantly, we had the impression that the Laotians were a gentle and civilized people who had no interest in killing each other.

There were very few significant battles when only Laotians
were on the battlefield without the presence of the North
Vietnamese. A few explosions made a big battle, there were
very few casualties. I remember one report that said that
the two Laotian sides left the battlefield on one occasion,
went to a water festival together, and then went back to
the battlefield. We decided that what we ought to work
for was a Laos which everyone would leave alone. We
would get out, the North Vietnamese would get out, the
French would get out, in order that the Laotians could
manage, or mismanage, their own affairs in whatever way
they wanted to. In the Laos Conference in 1961 and 1962
where the Peoples' Republic of China was represented by
their foreign minister, Mr. Chen Yi, we made some substantial concessions to get an agreement, at least concessions
in relation to the previous attitude of the Eisenhower administration. We accepted, for example, the Soviet nominee
as the Prime Minister of Laos, the present Prime Minister,
Prince Souvana Phouma. He was not our candidate, he
was the Soviet candidate. We accepted a coalition government, made up of the Right, the Communists, and the
Neutralists. We accepted the international neutralization
of Laos. But we got no performance on the agreement.
The North Vietnamese did not withdraw their forces, as
required by the agreement; they did not stop using Laos
as an infiltration route into South Vietnam, as required
by the agreement; they did not permit the coalition government or the International Control Commission to function
in those areas of Laos that were held by the Communists.
That bitter disappointment of 1962 and 1963 deeply affected President Kennedy's thinking.

During the Johnson years we had a somewhat different
problem. Peking was extremely harsh about Southeast Asian

matters. They made it impossible for us to take the question before the United Nations because they joined with Hanoi in saying that Vietnam was not a problem suitable to the United Nations, that it was not the business of the United Nations. That attitude lead people like Secretary General U Thant and a good many members of the U.N. to take the view that, under those circumstances, the U.N. should not take up the question. On a number of occasions, we counted noses behind the scenes and found that we did not have the votes even to put the question on the agenda. Similarly, the Chinese blocked on more than one occasion a reconvening of the Geneva Conferences in order to use that machinery to try to reach peace. It was clear that the Chinese were urging the North Vietnamese to continue the battle and press it forward to a military conclusion.

Secondly, during those same years, there developed a very important struggle for power inside China itself. You will remember the Red Guard Episode, the triangular tension between the old line Communist Party, the Red Guards and the armed forces. There were considerable periods when we did not know to whom to address a letter. The Red Guards, for example, were calling for the burning of my colleague, the foreign minister, Mr. Chen Yi. I got to be rather nervous about the idea of burning foreign ministers because I didn't want it to become contagious. But it was apparent in our bilateral talks in Warsaw that there really was not much opportunity for serious communication between the two sides. Bear in mind that from the middle 1950s up until fairly recently we have had regular bilateral talks through our ambassadors, first in Geneva and then in Warsaw; that we have probably had more direct diplomatic talks with the Peoples' Republic of China than any government that has formal relations with them, with the possible exception of the Soviet Union. But what we found out in those talks did not produce a positive result. We continued, for example, to propose such things as the exchange of newsmen, the exchange of scholars, scientists, and students, of cultural groups, of weather information; we offered to send them improved varieties of the basic food plants in which they were in desperate need; but, to sum it all up, in most of those talks they ended with the statement that there is nothing to discuss until we Americans were prepared to surrender Taiwan. Well, we took the view that Taiwan was not ours to surrender, that we could not come to terms on any such basis. So, during the Kennedy and Johnson years, except for probes that came to no result, there was very little movement in American-Chinese relations.

Then, we come to President Nixon's period; certain important things have happened that changed the situation somewhat. First, Mr. Nixon has made it clear, with the full approval, I think, of a majority of the American people, that we are withdrawing substantially from the western rim of the Pacific. We are getting out of Southeast Asia. The only serious argument about that is how quickly, and under what circumstances. But we are getting out. We are getting out of Taiwan over a period of time; we are reducing our forces in Korea, we have turned Okinawa back to the Japanese. So, undoubtedly, that major movement toward withdrawal from their own neighborhood has made some impact upon the Chinese. Secondly, the struggle for power inside China appears to be at least temporarily resolved and it apparently has become more possible for Mr. Chou En-lai to undertake active discussions, even with the arch-imperialist-capitalist country, the United States. Mr. Chou En-lai is a highly intelligent, sophisticated, worldly-wise man who knows how to handle himself in that kind of situation and opened the way for President Nixon's visit. Then, if I may tease my Republican friends just for a moment, the domestic politics of the situation changed somewhat. When Mr. Nixon goes to China, he only has the Democrats in opposition; if a Democratic president had gone to China, he would have had the Republicans in opposition. I think there is a considerable difference between those two situations on this issue. I have said to some of my Republican friends that when I recall what the Republican Party did to the Democrats from 1949 to 1952 over the China issue, I felt the Republicans had earned the right to find an answer to this question. But, in any event, President Nixon made his important visit to Peking. It opened up a number of questions about the future and I want to talk to you for a few minutes about some of those questions.

The most immediate question is whether his visit and the joint communiqué, which was issued at the time of his visit, will now be followed up by specific agreement, giving practical effect to those points which appeared to be agreed upon in principle. We do not know the answer to that question yet. Secretary Marshall used to tell us, "Never agree in principle, because all that means is that you haven't agreed yet." On such things as the exchange of newsmen, of cultural groups, of scientists or scholars, and improving trade, which seem to be accepted in the communiqué, there will have to be worked out a number of agreements, giving arms and legs to the general notion. In the trade field, it may be necessary for us to get certain legislation from the Congress, because it is hard to expect the Chinese to make any dent in our own market here under the terms of the old Smoot-Hawley Tariff. We would have to find some way to give them, if not most favored nations's treatment, at least more normal treatment, under conditions of present trading practices. Those details remain for the future.

I see no evidence that there has been any agreement between the two sides on such important questions as Southeast Asia or Taiwan. Let me hasten to say I have not been briefed on what went on in those talks; I have not asked for a briefing, so my information on that is about what yours is if you have read the papers and magazines rather carefully. The question is whether we can now expect to go into a period of probing for points of agreement.

Let me remind you that during the sixties, President Kennedy, and more particularly President Johnson, came to the conclusion that it was just too late in history for any two powers, particularly nuclear powers, to pursue a policy of total hostility toward each other. We began to explore for points of possible agreement, large or small, where the common interest of both countries might be engaged and might result in some sort of understanding on particular issues, not despite our differences on other questions, but because of those differences. A deliberate attempt has been made to lay some foundation of common interests which might, in the long run, put a restraining hand upon the nuclear beast which is the number one problem before the human race. I hope those probes with the Soviet Union will continue. For example, I do hope that President Nixon, in his forthcoming visit to Moscow, can find a basis for a significant agreement on nuclear offensive and defensive missiles. It may be that we now have a chance during the seventies to try the same kind of probing with the Chinese.

It may take time; it may be complicated; it may be frustrating.

Bear in mind that foreign policy is that part of our public business which we ourselves cannot control. The President, the Congress, the Supreme Court, our governors, state legislatures and local authorities can, by and large, determine what we do about our domestic affairs. But as soon as we step across a national frontier, we are dealing with some 140 other governments, each living in a different part of the world, each with its own problems, its own aspirations, its own policies; no one of which simply salutes when we speak. It is a world of negotiation, discussion, compromise, adjustment, sometimes pressure, and on rare occasions, unhappily, violence. Disappointment and frustration are built into the very process of foreign policy. It is one of the reasons why no one should ever expect the State Department to be popular among the American people. Among other things, it is the department of bad news. I would myself hope that some specific agreements can be reached reasonably soon with the Chinese even though they may turn out to be rather small at the beginning.

A second major question is what kind of a member will China now be in the United Nations and its specialized agencies? Will it pursue a positive and constructive policy as a member of the community of nations and try to work out agreement with the great majority of the members of the U.N., under the guidelines of the United Nations Charter, or will it be bitter and hostile and obstructive? We do not clearly know the answer to that question yet. My guess is that if the Chinese should enter the United Nations with the general spirit with which they went to the Bandung Conference in Indonesia, where they were friendly and cooperative and reasonable, they would find that there would be a place of considerable leadership waiting for them in the United Nations. But they could offend a great many of the members of the U.N. if they take the other tack. We will have a pretty good chance in the very near future to test that point because in June of this year there will convene in Stockholm a United Nations conference on the human environment and the People's Republic of China will be there. In 1973 there will convene a very important law of the sea conference to develop new rules about the territorial sea and the handling of the resources of the sea beds. Nineteen hundred and seventy-four has been designed "United Nations Population Year."

We have always the open question as to whether the Chinese will now become an active party in the continuing effort to find some limitation to the arms race. I would be glad to see them, for example, sign the test ban treaty; I would be glad to see them sign the nonproliferation treaty, neither of which they have yet signed. I would be glad to see them brought promptly into talks on the subjects that are now being discussed between us and the Russians in the so-called SALT talks. I would be glad to see them take an active part in the Geneva Conference on the limitation of arms. But we still have no clear answer to that question.

Another question is what attitude will China now take towards its own neighbors in Asia. I am thinking particularly of Japan and India and Southeast Asia. Will they continue to pursue a policy of militant world revolution, or will they try to move toward something that might realistically be called genuine peaceful coexistence? The answer to that is still unresolved.

In the background is the important question of Taiwan. There has been some confusion, it seems to me, about the Taiwan problem. I do not believe the people in Peking can claim Taiwan under such war-time declarations as the Cairo Declaration, which promised to return Taiwan to China. It seems to me those promises were completed by performance, because Taiwan was returned to those to whom we promised it during World War II. The separation of Taiwan from the mainland came about as the result of a civil war. Both sides claimed control over the other. I personally do not see any prospect of any significant change in that problem so long as Mao Tse-tung and Chiang Kai-shek are still with us. After the two of them leave the scene almost anything can happen, ranging from a wholly independent Taiwan under the domination of its own indigenous people, the Taiwanese, all the way to an absorption of Taiwan by mainland China. When our delegation came back from the talks in Peking considerable care was taken to state that the security treaty between us and Taiwan remains in full force and effect. Whether that was discussed in Peking we do not know. What the effect of that is for the future will depend upon the answers of people like you sitting in this room, because the validity of a security treaty depends on the understanding and support of the American people.

A further question is what the next generation of Chinese leaders will look like. We are now dealing with the second generation of leadership in the Soviet Union. Mr. Mikoyan was the last of the old Bolsheviks in the Soviet government. This new generation tends to be pragmatic, business-like, technocratic, direct, sometimes tough; the very exchanges between our two governments, between Washington and Moscow, have changed in character since the departure of Mr. Khrushchev and the other old Bolsheviks. You do not get long, ideological tirades anymore, the kinds of things you could write yourself before you get the answer, the sorts of things that come off mimeograph machines. Recent messages have been short and to the point, sometimes, of course, not agreeable, but to me that method of communication is already an improvement. In the case of the Chinese, we are still dealing with the original ideologues of the Long March. The acting President of China is now about eighty-nine, I believe; Mao Tse-tung is seventy-eight; Chou En-lai is about seventy-three. So a new generation of leaders will be there shortly, because even Chinese Communists are not immortal. Who will these people be? Maybe the Chinese themselves do not know. We ourselves do not know very much about what that second generation will look like. If they are younger people who will be more directly concerned with the problems of 800 million or a billion Chinese, if they are in an attitude to try to work out practical arrangements to make life possible between different political and social systems then, maybe, a great deal can be accomplished. If, on the other hand, they are a second generation of red-hot ideologists then we all may have some problems in front of us.

I have no doubt that our own relations with Peking will be influenced, to some extent, by the relations between Peking and Moscow. I do not know what those relations are. It does not embarrass me that I do not know, because I suspect that Peking and Moscow are not really sure about what those relations are. I am strongly convinced that it would be very unwise for the United States to try to play cute games in attempting to manipulate the Soviet Union and the People's Republic of China against each other. They are highly intelligent people. They will see through any such child's maneuver. The stakes that are involved in their own relations with each other are so great that our role in them can only be minimal. Bear in mind that these are two great Communist countries, and although they have had some pretty good family quarrels, they remain Communist countries. I do not underestimate the possibility that Moscow and Peking might, on some occasion, put aside their bilateral problems in order to combine in a joint program in direct support of what both of them call the world revolution. I do not believe those troubled waters are waters in which the United States should try to fish. I accept at face value the statement by President Nixon that he is not engaging in any such game, that what he is trying to do is to improve our relations both with the People's Republic of China and with the Soviet Union, and to resolve some of the questions which are so inflammatory in terms of the prospects for peace.

Finally, I would say that China is of extraordinary importance because of its size and weight. Was it Napoleon who said, "Let China sleep, for when she awakes, the world will tremble"? I once pointed out in Washington that very shortly there will be a billion Chinese, armed with nuclear weapons, and that we do not know what their policy will be ten or twenty years from now. One or two people, quite unworthily, charged me with raising the specter of the "yellow peril" on the basis of racial prejudice. I do not know anybody who does not think they will be armed with nuclear weapons. I do not know anyone who knows what their policy is going to be ten or twenty years from now.

But the family of man, within the next decade or two, is coming into being as an organic community, not through sentiments of brotherhood—unfortunately those sentiments are not pervasive enough, or deep enough, to bring about result—but because of the sheer necessity of solving certain problems around the end of this century if the human race is to survive. These problems are different in kind from any problems we have faced before in the long history of man. I have in mind such questions as nuclear weapons and the problem of nuclear war. The problem of war is a wholly different problem now than it was at any time up until the mid 1950s when a full nuclear exchange first became possible. I have in mind the problem of environment, because we are finding out that man himself can do very serious injury to the tiny skin around this fleck of dust in the Universe—a few inches of soil, two miles of air, three miles of ocean depth—on which the human race has to live. And I am thinking of the population problem. We'll have six and one-half to seven billion people by the end of the century, and if those curves continue at present rates the figures become literally impossible to think about after the turn of the century. I personally have considerable faith in the essential rationality of homo sapiens when he is confronted by a problem which must be solved for his own survival. In that family of man, there surely will have to be room for the Chinese. We must keep our wits about us and not subject ourselves to all sorts of illusions. We must be commonsensical, but we must also be prepared to see whether we and the Chinese can make more sense with each other, because the stakes are very high. I am glad President Nixon went to Peking. All the hard work still remains in front of us. A lot of it will depend upon the patience and the understanding of the American people in giving Mr. Nixon, or who ever else might be in that office, to chance to pursue these matters further.